Scandinavian Smorgasbord Recipe

Collected and edited by Karen Berg Douglas

Cover: Rogaland Rosemaling by Sallie Haugen DeReu
Associate editors: Miriam Canter, Dorothy Crum, Georgia
Dianne Stevens, and Joan Liffring-Zug Bourret

The traditional old country Scandinavian smorgasbords offered little more
butter, herring, dried prunes, apples, pickled beets, cabbage, beans, and pota
puddings and cookies for desserts. I've included a few updated recipes that
found on a Scandinavian smorgasbord today.
        —Kare

We wish to acknowledge:

The successful preparation of a smorgasbord often depends upon the use of authentic Scandinavian products. Recipes listing the following products: *Jarlsberg* Norwegian Cheese, *Nökkelost* Norwegian Cheese, *Gjetost* Norwegian Cheese; Kavli Norwegian Crispbreads; Classic Saga (blue) Cheese, Sage Mushroom Cheese, and Garlic/Chive Saga Cheese are provided through the courtesy of the makers and the Burrell Group, Ltd., Norseland Foods, Inc., and Tholstrup Cheese U.S.A.

We thank all contributors, who are noted throughout this book, for their part in providing a generous selection of *Scandinavian Smorgasbord Recipes.*

Please write for a complete listing of all our Scandinavian titles.

Table of Contents

About the Author and the Cover Artist

Karen Berg Douglas, of Finnish-Swedish heritage, learned the art of Scandinavian cookery from her Finnish-born mother. Karen's recipes have appeared in many cookbooks and periodicals. Many of these recipes come from her personal collection. A daily columnist and feature writer for the *Lansing State Journal* in Lansing, Michigan, she co-edited a Scandinavian cookbook for the Scandinavian Society of Greater Lansing.

The cover design and Rogaland pen and ink sketches by folk artist Sallie Haugen De Reus of Leighton, Iowa, are rooted in the traditions of Rogaland painting from the southwest coastal region of Norway. The American style of Rogaland painting is more precise and less spontaneous with more intense colors than those used in Norway. Sally was commissioned as one of several artists to create rosemaling at the EPCOT Center, Walt Disney World Vacation Kingdom's Norwegian Pavilion, Lake Buena Vista, Florida.

The Smorgasbord

The traditional Swedish smorgasbord, as we know it, can be found in all five Nordic countries. It just takes on a different name. In Denmark and Norway, it is known as the *Koldtbord*; in Finland, it is called the *Voileipäpöytä,* and in Iceland it is the *Kalt Bord*. Despite the different names, there is a similarity in observance, etiquette, and menu.

A long plain-cloth-covered table frequently serves as the background for an artistry of culinary delights in each of the five countries. Table decor may include fresh flowers and greens or candles, but the true beauty lies in the colorful variety of foods. Guests are invited to make frequent trips to the table, taking a clean plate for each course.

A variety of bread and butter is the mainstay of all smorgasbords. The first course includes a selection of pickled and preserved herring. Next comes the cold food

(continued)

5

course of smoked fish, meats, salads, and potatoes, then the hot foods, such as meatballs, fish dishes, and casseroles.

Scandinavians are known the world over for their wonderful desserts, and the best comes last. The dessert table is always laden with a wonderful array of cheese, cookies, cakes, and puddings.

A grand finale to a grand way to enjoy food!

A Danish *Koldtbord*

The name *koldtbord,* or cold table, is misleading, as hot dishes are frequently found on a Danish *koldtbord*. In addition, you're likely to find a beautiful array of Danish *smørrebrød*, delicate little open-faced sandwiches.

If I were to offer my friends a taste of my ethnicity, I'd serve helpings of many kinds of distinctly Danish joy—open-faced sandwiches for their beauty and variety; sago soup for its sweetness and texture; pickled herring for its piquant edge; meatballs for their substantial goodness; hot potato salad and red cabbage for balance and color; salmon and beet and onion salad to honor sea and land; rice pudding for contentment; apple cake for sensual pleasure, and vanilla wreaths for a crowning sweetness. That's how Danes cook, and that's how they live.

—Julie Jensen McDonald, author of *Delectably Danish: Recipes and Traditions*

A Finnish *Voileipäpöytä*

Visitors to the small Baltic Sea country of Finland will experience true Finnish hospitality in its *voileipäpöytä,* or bread and butter table. However, they should expect more than a simple sandwich. The Finns' love for good food and nature can be seen in a cornucopia of selections, including fish, meat, salad, and hot courses, all artfully arranged on the table.

The crisp, white linen tablecloth that my mother carried from her native Finland was a beautiful backdrop for many festive dinners in our home when I was a child. Fresh flowers, lighted candles, and linen napkins provided the color, along with an overwhelming variety of different foods.

Mama never wanted anyone to go away hungry because she didn't have something they liked. To my knowledge no one ever did.

—Karen Berg Douglas

Icelandic *Kalt Bord*

You may be baffled by the great variety of items on the cold buffet and wonder what to choose and where to start. It might help to know how we would do it in Iceland.

On our first round to the buffet, we would make a good selection from the herring varieties, which we take with rye bread and butter.

Returning to the buffet a second time, we would choose whatever looks tempting. Remember that you may return as often as you desire, and you may take a clean plate each time.

For dessert, we would have a good portion of *Skyr*, which we take with cream and sprinkle with sugar.

—Embassy of Iceland, Washington, D.C.

Norway's Breakfast Smorgasbords

When we came out of the mountains in the western part of Norway, we stayed at a ski resort. We had to wait in three tunnels for snowplows to bring us through. At this beautiful resort in Vagslid, the breakfast was a smorgasbord with the dishes on two levels. There were large wooden buckets of oatmeal—several kinds—served raw with milk and sugar, plus three other kinds of cereal. Different kinds of cheeses were offered, and many kinds of good, grainy Norwegian breads served with marmalade.

They had egg cups for the soft-boiled eggs; there was ham and dried mutton. Herring and mackerel were also offered. It was a first for us to have beet pickles for breakfast. The Norwegians serve foods so beautifully. They placed aluminum foil inside napkins to shape them like Viking ships.

—Thelma Bakken Hottel, Iowa City, Iowa

A Child's Discovery:
A Swedish-American Home Smorgasbord

I am thankful to have been raised in a Scandinavian neighborhood in northern Minnesota. My grandfather, a homesteader, was half-Norwegian, and my grandmother was of English descent. Nearly all of our neighbors were Swedish or Norwegian.

The closest our own home-cooked meals came to Norwegian was in servings of a lot of pickled herring and codfish. I was entranced by Mrs. Godfrey Lindquist and her wonderfully filled table holding every possible treat known to a home-baking, home-gardening Swedish woman.

Her round kitchen table with walleyed pike, ham, sliced beef or venison, cold soups, hot dishes, etc., was wonderful, and this was my introduction to the variety

(continued)

and wonder of Scandinavian cooking. As we ate, she would keep thinking of other treats she had forgotten to serve, and she would bring it to the table even if she had to go to the basement to find it among her many shelves of home-canned goodies.

Our family's little poodle made a daily trek to her back door, almost a quarter-mile away, to see if any table scraps were available. Now, a half-century later, writing about her cooking makes me ache with longing.

—Joan Liffring-Zug Bourret

A Smorgasbord Menu

Herring Anchovies Sardines Smoked Salmon
Pickles Olives Radishes Cucumbers
Jams and Jellies
Meatballs Assorted Cheeses Cold Meats
Herring Salad Sliced Tomatoes Pickled Beets
Baked Beans Potatoes
Rice Pudding Lingonberries Rolls and Breads
Fruitcake Cookies
Coffee

An Arctic Ice Sculpture

Looking for a unique item for your table?

Create an "Arctic Ice Sculpture" by placing a bottle of Finlandia Vodka in an empty milk carton. Then fill the carton with water and freeze until solid. The vodka itself will not freeze. To remove the sculpture, run lukewarm water around the outside of the carton. The bottle will emerge in a beautiful icy chunk which will last quite a while for your guests to admire.

For an even more exotic centerpiece, drop long-stemmed flowers of varying heights into a container before freezing for a gorgeous "ice flower" display.

Then line a tray or large crystal bowl with colorful cloth napkins; place the Finlandia ice block on top, and serve with a rousing toast of *Kippis!*—to your good health!

—Finnish National Distillers (ALKO), Inc.

Appetizers — Beverages

Herring:

More Appetizers:

Beverages:

Glass Master's Herring

Finnish

Marinade:
1 1/4 cups vinegar
1 1/4 cups sugar
2 1/2 cups water

4 large herring
3 red onions
2 carrots
15 whole allspice
15 white peppercorns
4 bay leaves

Marinade: In a saucepan, bring all ingredients to a boil. Allow to cool at room temperature.

Herring: Soak the fish overnight in cold water. Water should be changed periodically. Gut fish. Rinse well and dry with paper towel. Cut into sections. Peel the onions and carrots and cut into rings. Fill large glass jar with alternate layers of fish slices, onions, carrots, and the spices. Pour liquid over all. Cover jar and store in a cool place for at least two days.

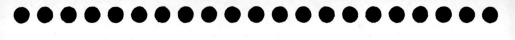

Matjes Herring
Swedish

1 can matjes herring
dill sprigs

1/4 cup chopped chives
1 cup sour cream

Drain the herring and cut into serving pieces. Slide a spatula under the herring and transfer to an oblong serving dish so that the fillets look whole. Chill and garnish with dill sprigs, if desired. Serve with chopped chives and sour cream. Hot new dill potatoes, sliced green pepper, and sliced red or yellow onion may also be served with matjes herring.

—Embassy of Sweden, Washington, D.C.

Mustard Herring

Danish

3 marinated herring
2 tablespoons dry mustard
2 tablespoons sugar
dash salt

dash white pepper
1 tablespoon white vinegar
1 pint whipping cream, whipped
dill weed

Cut up herring. Arrange on platter. Mix spices, seasonings, and vinegar. Fold in whipped cream. Place a spoonful on each piece of herring. Sprinkle with dill.

—Else Lassiter, *Delectably Danish: Recipes and Traditions*

Pickled Herring

Danish

2 herring, filleted and skinned
2 medium-sized onions, sliced
1/2 cup white vinegar

2/3 cup water
1 cup sugar
3/4 teaspoon allspice

Soak fillets in cold water for 24 hours. Drain and rinse. Cut into 1/2-inch pieces. Place in a glass jar. Combine remaining ingredients and bring to a boil. Cool and pour over herring. Refrigerate overnight before serving.

Pickled Herring

Swedish

8 salt herring, bone removed
3 cups milk
3 medium-sized onions, thinly sliced
pepper

1/2 cup sugar
1 cup white vinegar
1 cup water

Slice boned herring in half lengthwise and soak in milk overnight in refrigerator. Drain and rinse herring and cut into 1/2-inch pieces. Place alternate layers of herring and thinly sliced onion into a shallow dish; sprinkle each layer with pepper. Dissolve sugar in the vinegar and add water. Mix well and pour over herring and onions. Refrigerate several hours before serving.

Crusty Stuffed Bread

1 loaf Italian or French bread, about
    14 inches long
4 ounces Classic Saga blue cheese,
    broken into small pieces
1/3 cup black olives, sliced and pitted
1 tomato, diced

1 small red onion, finely chopped
1 small dill gherkin, chopped
1 tablespoon olive oil
1 tablespoon red wine vinegar
1 teaspoon oregano, crumbled

With a serrated knife, cut bread in half lengthwise. Remove soft white inside and
crumble into a large bowl. In the bowl, stir in Saga cheese and remaining ingredients.
Blend well. Place mixture into bottom half of bread shell and replace top. Bake in a
preheated oven (350°) for 20 to 25 minutes or until crusty. Cut into diagonal slices
to serve. Bread can also be served cold without baking.

Danish Liver Paste

1 pound liver
1 pound lean salt pork
1 medium-sized onion
1 tablespoon sugar
3 tablespoons flour

1 egg
1 tablespoon anchovy paste
pepper to taste
1 cup milk

Scald the liver and cook gently for 5 minutes, then put through a food chopper together with the pork and onion. Make a smooth paste. Add remaining ingredients and the milk, a little at a time. Mix well. Put into 9x5x3-inch loaf pan. Place pan into another pan with about 1 inch of warm water on the bottom. Bake at 350° for about 1 hour or until done.

Finnish Squeaky Cheese

This mild cheese (juusto) *can be served as an appetizer on the smorgasbord or with afternoon coffee. It makes a "squeak" when chewed.*

2 1/2 gallons milk
1 tablespoon cool water
1/2 rennet tablet*

1 tablespoon cornstarch
1 tablespoon salt
1 tablespoon sugar

Heat milk in double boiler to 88° but not over 90°. Dissolve crushed rennet in 1 tablespoon cool water; set aside. In a cup, mix dry ingredients with a small amount of the warmed milk. Add this and dissolved rennet to warm milk. Stir well; set aside to jell. Do not disturb. Jelling time varies, 20 to 45 minutes. Test by inserting wooden spoon into mixture. When jellied properly the spoon should leave a clean hole. When

(continued)

Finnish Squeaky Cheese   *(continued)*

jelled, stir to break up curds into chunks, about 1 inch. Let set 5 to 10 minutes until whey separates from curds. Drape a thin wet cloth over a bowl. Pour jelled mixture onto the cloth; gather all corners and squeeze out as much whey as possible. Press curds firmly into a 9-inch round pan, without cloth, and bake at 400° for 15 minutes. Periodically pour off whey. Broil on both sides until light golden brown. Cool on a rack and let dry 1 to 2 hours. Refrigerate.

—A Finn Fest Recipe

*Rennet tablets can be found in drugstores.

Nökkelost Pumpernickel Rounds

8 slices party pumpernickel bread
1/2 cup shredded *nökkelost* cheese
3 tablespoons softened butter or
  margarine

2 teaspoons red currant jelly
3 tablespoons finely chopped walnuts
4 apricot halves: fresh, canned, or
  dried

With a scalloped cookie cutter, cut bread slices into largest circles possible. In small bowl, blend *nökkelost* cheese and butter until smooth. Spread on 4 rounds of bread. Place another slice on top of each. Spread around sides. Roll sides in walnuts to coat. Spread remaining cheese mixture on top of sandwiches. Place apricot in center of each and top with a dollop of jelly. Sprinkle remaining nuts around edge of apricots.

Nutty Cheese Crispies

Norwegian

1 cup shredded *Jarlsberg* Lite cheese
1/2 cup sliced natural almonds
1/2 teaspoon ground cumin

pinch of cayenne red pepper
1 cup prepared salsa

Toss together cheese, almonds, cumin, and pepper. Drop in mounds, about 1 tablespoon each, onto nonstick baking sheet. Bake at 350° for 12 to 15 minutes, until cheese is golden brown. Remove from oven and allow crispies to cool on baking sheet. Arrange on serving plate and offer a bowl of salsa for dipping.

Oysters Helsinki

6 chilled oysters: shucked,
  left in the half shell
Finlandia vodka

3 teaspoons sour cream
Beluga caviar

Pour 1/4 ounce Finlandia vodka over each oyster. Spoon 1/2 teaspoon chilled sour cream over each oyster. Garnish with Beluga caviar. Serve chilled, on ice, accompanied by an icy cold shot of Finlandia vodka.

—Recipe created by Chef Michael Speranza
Horizon Restaurant at the Lodge at Woodcliff
Rochester, New York

Scandia Sardine Spread

Norwegian

1 3 3/4-ounce can of King Oscar
   sardines in oil, drained
1/2 cup (about 2 ounces) shredded
   Swiss or Monterey Jack cheese
1/4 cup sliced green onions

2 tablespoons Dijon-style mustard
1 tablespoon lemon juice
1 teaspoon grated lemon peel
2 ounces chopped pimientos
parsley, chopped
1 lemon, sliced

In a mixing bowl, mash sardines lightly with a fork. Add remaining ingredients and mix thoroughly. Garnish with the chopped parsley and lemon slices. Serve with crackers or snack bread.

Danish Wine Cooler

4 fresh orange slices
1 lemon, sliced
1/4 cup sugar

1/4 cup brandy
1 26-ounce bottle white wine, chilled
1 12-ounce bottle club soda, chilled

Place fruit in a large glass pitcher. Sprinkle with sugar. Add brandy; chill 2 to 3 hours, then add ice and wine. Add club soda just before serving. Serves 12.

Finnish Coffee

8 cups water
6 tablespoons ground coffee

1 egg, slightly beaten
dash of salt

Heat water in glass or porcelain enamel coffee pot. Mix coffee grounds with about 1 tablespoon of the slightly beaten egg. When water begins to boil, add coffee ground-egg mixture and cook for 4 to 5 minutes. Remove from heat; sprinkle a few grains of salt in the pot and allow to stand for 3 to 4 hours until grounds settle to the bottom of the pot. Serve at once.

—Karen Berg Douglas

Finnish May Day Drink

4 quarts water
2 1/3 cups light brown sugar
1/4 cup honey
1 lemon

grated lemon rind
1/8 teaspoon dry yeast
1/2 cup golden raisins

Bring water to a boil. Add the sugar, honey, and finely shredded lemon rind. Cool. Remove the white part of the lemon and slice the lemon into thin slices. Dissolve yeast in 1 tablespoon warm water. Add yeast and lemon slices to the mixture. Let stand at room temperature until completely cooled. Add the raisins and pour into sterilized jars or bottles with screw-on tops. Chill for 3 to 5 days before serving. Continue to refrigerate. Makes 1 gallon.

—Luela Maki, Ely, Minnesota

Kaffe Smoothie

8 well-rounded tablespoons coffee
1/2 cup coffee-flavored liqueur
1/2 cup light cream or half and half

1/8 teaspoon cinnamon
3 cups cold water

Place coffee in the basket of an automatic drip coffeemaker. Put liqueur, cream, and cinnamon into the pot of the coffeemaker. Using the 3 cups of water prepare coffee as directed. Stir well and serve hot. Serves 4.

—Gevalia Kaffe

Mountain Ash Liqueur

1 cup frostbitten mountain ash berries　　1 cup sugar
1 liter strong, clear unspiced alcohol　　1 cup water
　(such as vodka)

Wash berries and remove stems. Crush berries in a large bowl and pour alcohol over them. Place in tightly closed sterilized glass jar and let stand for 2 to 3 weeks. Strain when the berries have become lighter in color and the liquid has absorbed their flavor. Put the berries in a jelly bag or a piece of cheesecloth and squeeze all the juice from them into the strained liqueur. Boil the sugar and water until clear; cool and add to the berry juice liqueur. Serve cold with ice.

Note: The liqueur gets smoother if you let it stand for a few weeks in a cool place.

—Ritva Kamrin, East Lansing, Michigan

Reindeer Tears

Finnish

whole cranberries   vodka

Place 2 or 3 whole cranberries into a 2-ounce cordial or liqueur glass. Fill with vodka, say *"Kippis!"* (to your good health) and drink up!

—Aimo Tervakoski, *Fantastically Finnish: Recipes and Traditions*

Kalja

Finnish

1 cup rye malt   5 quarts boiling water
1 cup sugar   1 teaspoon yeast

Mix malt and sugar in a large saucepan and pour boiling water on top. When the water has cooled to the touch, add yeast. Cover pan and allow the *Kalja* to ferment overnight. The following day, strain liquid and pour into bottles. Keep in a cool place.

Scandinavian Fruit Glogg

1 quart apple cider
juice of 1 orange
2 cups grape juice
1/4 cup sugar

2 cinnamon sticks
6 cloves
1/3 cup raisins
1/3 cup blanched almonds

In a 30-cup automatic coffeemaker, combine cider, juice from 1 orange, grape juice, and sugar. In the basket of the coffeemaker, place cinnamon sticks and cloves. Bring to a boil, so it cooks like coffee. Serve hot over a few raisins and almonds placed in each glass coffee cup. Makes 12 to 14 servings.

Scandinavian Spiced Mead Honey Wine

5 pounds honey
4 quarts water
3 tablespoons whole cloves
3 tablespoons cassia buds

1/4 pound candied ginger, finely
   chopped
1 package dry granulated yeast

Combine water and honey in a kettle and bring to a rolling boil. Boil for 10 minutes. Skim froth that rises to the surface. Place cloves and cassia buds into a small muslin bag and drop into the boiling liquid for the last 5 minutes of boiling. Remove from heat and add candied ginger. Set aside and cool to lukewarm. When lukewarm, sprinkle dry yeast over the surface and put in a warm place to ferment for 2 weeks. (Leave all spices in mead during this fermentation.) No stirring is necessary.

(continued)

Scandinavian Spiced Mead Honey Wine *(continued)*

After 2 weeks, strain through several thicknesses of cheesecloth; return to kettle to settle for 1 week. Siphon into clean sterilized bottles and cork loosely. When all fermentation has stopped, cork tightly and seal with paraffin. Let set for 3 months before using.

Swedish Christmas Punch

1 bottle Aquavit
1 bottle dry red wine
10 to 12 cardamom seeds
6 whole cloves
3 pieces dried orange peel

2 cinnamon sticks
1/2 pound sugar cubes
1 cup blanched almonds
1 cup raisins

Pour liquor and wine into a large pan. Add remaining ingredients, except sugar cubes. Cover and heat slowly to a boiling point. Remove from heat. Place sugar cubes in a metal sieve with a long handle; dip into hot liquid to moisten, then light sugar with a match and allow to burn. Dip sieve into liquid until sugar has melted into punch. Cover kettle to put out flame. Cool punch; pour into bottles and cap. Heat punch before serving but do not boil. Serve hot in glass mugs. Place a few raisins and almonds in each mug.

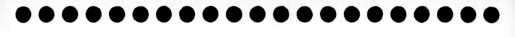

Swedish Glogg

1 bottle red wine
1/4 cup sugar
1/3 cup vodka
2 slices fresh ginger
2 cinnamon sticks

1/2 teaspoon cardamon seeds
5 to 7 whole cloves
1/2 cup raisins
3 tablespoons blanched almonds

Combine wine, sugar, vodka, ginger, and other spices in a large saucepan. Heat to simmer. Remove from heat, cover, and let stand 3 to 4 hours. To serve, heat glogg but do not boil. Place a few raisins and almonds in glass mugs or cups; pour hot glogg over them and serve. Serves 4 to 6.

Breads

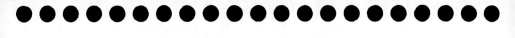

Adeline Stoor's Rye Bread

Swedish

4 cups warm water
2 packages dry yeast
1/3 cup sugar
1 tablespoon salt
1/4 cup melted shortening
1/2 cup dark molasses

1/2 cup dark corn syrup
1/2 teaspoon anise seeds
1/2 teaspoon caraway seeds
3 cups rye flour
6 1/2 cups white flour
2 tablespoons melted butter or
margarine

Sprinkle yeast in warm water; let stand until dissolved. Add sugar, salt, melted shortening, molasses, syrup, anise seed, caraway seed, rye flour, and 1 1/2 cups white flour. Beat with wooden spoon until smooth for about 2 minutes. Gradually add the rest of the white flour. Knead with hand until dough leaves side of bowl. Turn dough onto lightly floured board.

41   *(continued)*

Adeline Stoor's Rye Bread *(continued)*

Knead until smooth, about 10 minutes. Place in a greased bowl. Turn dough to bring up greased side. Cover with a damp cloth. Let rise in a warm place free of drafts, until doubled, about 1 hour. Grease three 9x3x5-inch loaf pans. Punch down dough. Turn out on a lightly floured surface. Shape into 3 loaves and place in loaf pans. Cover and let rise until doubled. Bake in a preheated oven at 375° for about 45 minutes. Remove to wire rack. Brush tops with melted butter or margarine.

—Pearl Stoor, Dollar Bay, Michigan

Esther's Danish Rye Bread

1 teaspoon yeast
1/4 cup warm water
1 quart buttermilk
3 tablespoons molasses

3 tablespoons lard
3 tablespoons salt
6 cups rye graham flour
6 cups whole-wheat flour

Soften yeast in warm water. Heat buttermilk until lukewarm. Mix in all ingredients and knead. Let stand overnight, covered. Punch down in the morning. Divide into 3 loaves and let rise in 9x5-inch loaf pans for 10 minutes. Place cookie sheet over pans with a weight on top while baking. Bake at 400° for about 10 minutes, then at 250° for 1 3/4 hours. Slice bread very thin for serving.

—Esther Andersen, Dike, Iowa
From *Delectably Danish: Recipes and Traditions*

Flat Bread

Icelandic

4 cups rye flour   1 1/4 cups boiling water

Moisten flour with the boiling water and knead. Divide dough into parts big enough to make thin, round cakes about the size of a dessert plate. Bake on a hot, cast-iron griddle, and turn frequently. Spread with butter. Good with smoked lamb, pâté, cheese, or smoked herring.

Note: Rye flour may be mixed with white flour, if preferred.

—Embassy of Iceland, Washington, D.C.

Finnish Flat Bread

1 3-ounce package dry yeast
2 cups warm water

1 teaspoon salt
4 1/2 to 5 cups rye or whole-wheat flour

Dissolve yeast in warm water. Combine salt and 2 cups of the flour. Stir in dissolved yeast. Continue to add flour until stiff. Turn out onto a lightly floured surface and knead until smooth and elastic, about 10 minutes. Place in a greased mixing bowl, cover with a damp cloth, and let rise until doubled. Turn out again onto a lightly floured surface and divide into 4 portions, shaping each into a ball. On a greased cookie sheet roll out each part to 1/4-inch thickness. Cut a hole in the center with a biscuit cutter. Prick entire surface with a fork. Bake at 450° for 15 minutes. Allow to dry, uncovered, overnight.

Graham Bread

Finnish

2 packages dry yeast
1/2 cup lukewarm water
4 cups milk
1/4 cup brown sugar

4 teaspoons salt
1/4 cup shortening
2 cups graham flour
8 cups white flour, divided

Dissolve yeast in lukewarm water. Scald milk and add sugar, salt, and shortening. Cool to lukewarm. Add graham flour. Add yeast mixture. Mix well. Add 6 cups white flour and stir to blend ingredients. On a floured surface, knead in the last 2 cups of flour to make a smooth and elastic dough, about 10 minutes. Put in greased bowl and cover with a towel. Let rise until doubled. Place on a floured surface and divide into 4 parts. Shape into loaves and transfer to greased loaf pans or shape into round balls for cookie sheets. Let rise for an hour. Bake at 375° for 35 to 40 minutes.

Hardtack

Swedish

4 cups oatmeal
1 cup flour
1/2 teaspoon soda

1/2 cup sugar
1/2 cup butter, melted
1 cup milk

Combine all ingredients. Let stand in a cool place overnight. Roll out dough very thin.
Cut into desired shapes and bake at 350° for 10 to 15 minutes or until done.

Leaf Bread

This bread is served with smoked lamb at Christmas time in northern and eastern Iceland.

1 teaspoon baking powder
4 cups flour
1 tablespoon butter

1 tablespoon sugar
1 cup hot milk
oil for deep-frying

Sift flour and baking powder together. Stir in the butter. Add sugar and moisten with the hot milk. Stir until mixture forms a dough. On a floured surface, knead until smooth. Divide into equal parts. Roll out until very thin and cut into rounds with a cake-cutting wheel. Keep in a cool place for 30 minutes, then cut decorative designs into each cake with a sharp knife and deep-fry until golden brown.

—Embassy of Iceland, Washington, D.C.

Norwegian Lefse

2 quarts mashed potatoes
1 tablespoon lard
1/2 teaspoon salt

3 tablespoons milk
flour as needed

Mix potatoes, lard, and salt in large bowl. Heat milk and stir into the mixture. Add enough flour to knead dough well, then take a piece of dough the size of an egg and roll out thin on lightly floured board. Bake on a preheated, ungreased hot griddle. Turn when brown. Fold each cake in half, then in thirds, and place on serving platter.

Old-Fashioned Clove Bread

Danish

2 cups lukewarm water
2 tablespoons yeast
2 teaspoons salt
1/3 cup maple syrup
4 tablespoons oil
2 teaspoons ground cloves

2 teaspoons ground ginger
4 1/2 to 5 cups whole wheat flour or
    half unbleached white and half
    whole-wheat flour
milk for brushing
poppy seeds for top

Dissolve yeast in milk. Add remaining ingredients; knead dough thoroughly. Let rise in warm place about 15 minutes. Divide dough in 2 parts and roll in 20-inch lengths. Twist the long rolls together. Let rise about 20 minutes. Brush with milk, sprinkle with poppy seeds, and bake on a greased baking sheet at 375° about 45 minutes.

—Birte Lund, Funen, Denmark
From *Delectably Danish: Recipes and Traditions*

Rye Bread Rolls

Finnish

3 cups water
25 pieces Finn Crisp or other rye crispbread
1 stick unsalted butter, softened

1 tablespoon prepared mustard
1 tablespoon chopped fresh dill
1/2 pound grated Emmenthaler cheese

Bring water to a boil and briefly dip each piece of crispbread in it, using a large slotted spoon or tongs. Place on waxed paper. In a small bowl, combine softened butter with mustard and dill. Spread some of the mixture over each piece of softened bread and cover with grated cheese. Roll up bread pieces and arrange on serving dish, seam side down. Cover with plastic wrap and refrigerate a few hours before serving.

—Finnish National Distillers (ALKO), Inc.

Sourdough Pumpernickel

Danish

Sourdough:
1 cup yeast dough (any kind)
2 1/2 cups lukewarm water
1/2 cup rye meal

Pumpernickel:
1 cake yeast
6 1/4 cups lukewarm water, divided
1/4 cup salt
4 cups rye graham or white flour
12 cups rye meal

Sourdough: Blend yeast dough with the lukewarm water and rye meal. Let stand overnight at room temperature.

Pumpernickel: Dissolve yeast in 1/4 cup of the lukewarm water. Mix yeast, sourdough, salt, 6 cups water, and flours. Mix well and let rise for 2 hours. Knead down and let stand for 15 minutes. Shape into loaves and let rise again for about 20 minutes. Bake at 375° for 1 1/2 to 1 3/4 hours. Makes three 2 1/2-pound halves.

—From *Delectably Danish: Recipes and Traditions*

Swedish Rye Bread

1 package active dry yeast
1/2 cup warm water
1 tablespoon fennel seeds
1 tablespoon anise seeds
1 teaspoon salt

2 tablespoons sugar
2 tablespoons butter, melted
2 cups milk, scalded and cooled
3 cups rye flour
3 to 3 1/2 cups all-purpose flour

Dissolve yeast in warm water; set aside 5 minutes. Crush fennel and anise seeds into a powder. Add powdered seeds, salt, sugar, butter, milk, and rye flour to yeast mixture; beat well. Add enough flour to mixture to make a stiff dough. Let rest for 15 minutes. Turn dough onto floured surface and knead until smooth, about 10 minutes. Grease large bowl. Place dough in bowl and turn once so greased side is up. Cover and let rise until doubled in bulk, about 2 hours. Punch dough down and divide into 4 parts. Shape each piece into a ball. Place balls on 2 greased baking sheets. Let rise about 1 hour. Bake at 375° for 25 minutes or until done. Cool on racks.

Esther Sater's Raisin-Nut Bread

This recipe was given to my mother by the late Ester Sater, daughter of the late Rev. August P. Sater, who founded Grace Lutheran Church in Lansing, Michigan, as well as several other Lutheran churches in Michigan.

–Karen Berg Douglas

1 1/2 cups raisins
1 1/2 cups water
3/4 cup raisin cooking liquid
1/2 cup brown sugar
1/2 cup white sugar
1 tablespoon butter

2 eggs
1 teaspoon salt
1 teaspoon vanilla
2 3/4 cups white flour
3 level teaspoons baking soda
1 cup coarsely chopped nuts

Boil raisins in the 1 1/2 cups of water. Drain 3/4 cup of the liquid into a large bowl; discard the rest. Then, cream the sugars and butter together. Add the eggs and mix

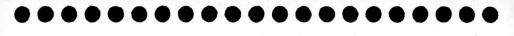

thoroughly. Stir in salt, vanilla, flour, and baking soda. Add the raisins and the nuts. Grease four 10 3/4-ounce cans (soup can size) and fill half-full with the batter. Bake at 325° for 1 hour. Allow to cool, then remove the breads carefully from cans and wrap each roll in waxed paper. (These can also be frozen wrapped in freezer wrap.) To serve, cut in thin slices and spread with cream cheese or pimiento cheese spread for attractive and delicious little party sandwiches.

Norwegian Coffee Bread

4 tablespoons butter	1 cup lukewarm milk
4 tablespoons shortening	1/2 cup currants
1 1/2 cups sugar	1/2 cup candied fruit peel
1/4 teaspoon salt	1 teaspoon crushed cardamom seeds
2 eggs	(optional)
2 cakes of yeast	3 1/2 cups flour (approximately)
	powdered sugar icing

Melt shortening; stir in sugar, salt, eggs, and cardamom (if desired). Dissolve yeast in warm milk. Add flour and the milk mixture, alternately, to batter. Mix well. Add currants and candied fruit peel. Let rise in a warm place until very light, about 2 hours. Knead down on floured surface and shape into two 12-inch braids. Place on baking sheet and let rise again until light. Bake at 375° for about 20 to 25 minutes. When cool, frost with powdered sugar icing.   56

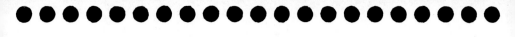

Swedish Almond Toast

1 cup butter
2 cups sugar
2 eggs
3 1/2 cups flour
2 teaspoons baking powder

1 cup sour cream
1 cup finely chopped almonds
2 teaspoons ground cardamon
1/4 teaspoon salt

Cream butter and sugar together in a large bowl. Add eggs and beat well. Add dry ingredients, sour cream, almonds, cardamon, and salt. Mix well. Spread in an ungreased jellyroll pan. Bake at 350° for 35 to 40 minutes, until brown. Cool in the pan. When cool, cut into small squares. Place squares on a cookie sheet and bake at 200° for about 1 1/2 hours until crisp.

Swedish Tea Ring

1 cake of yeast
1/4 cup lukewarm water
1 cup scalded milk
3/4 teaspoon salt
1/4 cup sugar
6 tablespoons shortening

3 1/2 cups sifted white flour, divided
1 egg, beaten
2 tablespoons melted butter
1/2 cup finely chopped nuts
powdered sugar and milk glaze
candied cherries and nuts for garnish

Soften yeast in water. Combine milk, salt, sugar, and shortening in pan and heat until lukewarm. Add yeast mixture and half the flour; beat well with a wooden spoon. Let rise until very light, about 1 hour. Then add the egg and remaining flour and mix well. Let rise again for about an hour. On a lightly floured surface, roll dough into a 3/8-

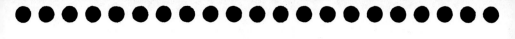

inch-thick rectangle. Brush with melted butter and sprinkle with 1/2 cup of finely chopped nuts. Roll up like a jellyroll, lengthwise; place on a greased baking sheet and form into a ring. Pinch ends together. Make partial cuts around the outside of the ring at 2-inch intervals (about two-thirds into ring). Turn each slice so it lies flat on the pan. Bake about 30 minutes at 400°. Brush with a powdered sugar and milk glaze and garnish with candied cherries and nuts.

—Marie Knight, Apache Jct., Arizona

Open-Faced Sandwiches

●●●●●●●●●●●●●●●●●●●●●●●●

The Swedish *Smörgås*

Swedes seldom eat a plain piece of bread with their meal. They would much rather eat *smörgås*–a small open-faced sandwich made with meat, fish, or cheese. And who wouldn't?

Smörgås is a diminutive form of the famed smorgasbord. It's nourishing and appetizing, and can easily be enjoyed with morning coffee, as a quick lunch, or as a between-meal snack.

Smörgås is one of the popular items found on the traditional Swedish smorgasbord.

Shrimp *Smörgås*

4 slices white or rye bread
butter
lettuce leaves
4 hard-cooked eggs, sliced
fresh cooked shrimp
radish slices and fresh dill for garnish

Dressing:
2 tablespoons mustard
1 tablespoon red wine vinegar
1/4 cup chili sauce
1/2 cup oil
salt and pepper to taste

Butter bread generously and trim crust from bread. Cover bread with lettuce and sliced eggs. Peel shrimp and place on top of each bread slice. Mix ingredients for dressing and pour over sandwiches. Garnish with radish slices and dill. Makes 4 sandwiches.

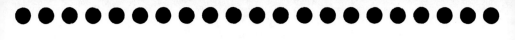

Herring *Smörgås*

dark rye bread
butter
mayonnaise
curry powder

hard-cooked egg, chopped
lettuce
herring tidbits in tomato sauce
fresh dill sprigs

Spread bread generously with butter, so liquid from fish mixture will not seep through. Season mayonnaise with curry to taste and blend with chopped egg. Put small leaf of lettuce on bread and cover with egg mixture. Arrange herring on top. Garnish with dill.

Danish *Smørrebrød*

Smørrebrød, or open-faced sandwiches, is a Danish luncheon staple, and the mainstay of easy, elegant entertainment. The little sandwiches, prepared with culinary artistry, are eaten with a knife and fork.

There are no hard-and-fast rules to the preparation of *smørrebrød*. It is left to the time and imagination of the creator.

First, the base: thin slices of dark rye or white bread, generously buttered and covered with a leaf of lettuce. It is necessary to cover the entire slice of bread with butter to keep moist toppings from soaking through. Cover one corner with a leaf of lettuce. Use plenty of topping so no bread shows.

Top with a variety of: herring, salami, roast beef, liver pâté, caviar, shrimp, cheeses, oysters, anchovies, crab, hard-cooked eggs, or sardines.

Garnish with selections of: thin slices of radish or cucumber; parsley, watercress, tomato slices, or cherry tomatoes, fresh fruit, sliced hard-cooked eggs, dill, chives, or olives.

Possible combinations:
White bread and lox, mayonnaise, and sweet pickles; chopped chicken, pineapple, and mayonnaise; chopped shrimp, cucumber slices, French dressing, and radishes; lobster and asparagus mixed with mayonnaise; rye bread with thinly sliced roast beef, cream cheese, and raw onion rings; liver pâté, sautéed mushrooms, strips of bacon, and lettuce; Danish blue cheese, onion rings, and sieved hard-cooked eggs; sliced corned beef, watercress, and sliced hard-cooked eggs; chopped and cooked chicken liver, crumbled bacon, sliced tomatoes, and lemon juice; sliced pork roast, prunes, and sliced oranges; sliced boiled new potatoes, bacon strips, cocktail sausages, tomato slivers, and chopped parsley.

Norwegian *Smørbrød*

8 ounces light cream cheese
1 tablespoon lemon juice
1/2 teaspoon dill weed
6 thick, or rye-bran style, Kavli
  Norwegian crispbreads

6 thin slices lean, smoked ham
6 Calimyrna figs, sliced
1 cup sliced cucumber rounds
fresh dill sprigs, optional

Mix together cream cheese, lemon juice, and dill weed. To assemble sandwiches, spread 2 tablespoons cream mixture on each crispbread. Top each with 1 slice ham, 1 sliced fig, and 3 to 4 slices cucumber. Garnish with dill. Makes 6 servings.

Blue Cheese Rounds

4 slices pumpernickel bread
4 ounces Classic Saga cheese,
   softened
1/2 cup alfalfa sprouts

1/4 cup chopped nuts (hazelnuts,
   almonds, or walnuts)

With a 2-inch cookie cutter, cut circles from bread slices. Spread with blue cheese. Cover edges with alfalfa sprouts and fill center with nuts. Refrigerate. Makes 8 rounds.

Chive Cheese with Smoked Salmon

4 slices toasted whole wheat bread
1/4 pound Saga chive cheese
1/4 pound sliced smoked salmon

capers
chives or dill for garnish

Trim crusts from bread. Cut into triangles or rectangles. Arrange a slice of cheese on each slice of bread. Roll up salmon slices, forming "roses," and place on sandwiches. Garnish with capers and chives. Makes 8 sandwiches.

Cucumber and Cheese

rye bread
butter
Cheddar cheese, sliced

cucumber
fresh parsley, chopped

Spread rye bread with butter. Trim crust from bread. Cover with cheese. Cut into 2 triangles. Garnish with a thin slice of cucumber and a sprig of parsley.

Salami and Cheese

knäckebröd or crispbread, cut into
  rectangles
butter

salami
Swiss cheese
fresh parsley, chopped

Spread rectangle of crispbread with butter. Cover with 2 slices of salami. Top with Swiss cheese and add sprig of parsley for color.

Garlic-Chive Shrimp Rounds

4 slices toasted whole wheat bread
1/4 pound Saga garlic/clove cheese
8 to 12 small cooked shrimp, halved
   lengthwise

lettuce
lemon slices

Using a cookie cutter, cut bread slices into 2-inch rounds. Slice cheese and arrange on bread. Top with shrimp; garnish with lettuce and lemon.

Knäckebröd and Cheese

knäckebröd or crispbread
butter
lettuce

Finnish *Lappi* cheese, sliced
radishes
parsley

Butter crispbread. Top with lettuce and slice of Finnish *Lappi* cheese. Garnish with radishes and parsley.

Nökkelost Open-Faced Sandwich

6 slices Kavli Norwegian thick flatbread
2 tablespoons softened butter or margarine
3 slices ham
3 slices roast beef
6 pieces Boston lettuce
green onions

cucumber slices
cherry tomatoes, halved
green pepper strips
radish rosettes
sweet gherkins
1/4 pound *nökkelost* cheese

Spread Kavli Norwegian thick flatbread with butter. Arrange ham and roast beef slices on individual flatbreads. Top each with lettuce. Decorate each of the flatbreads with assorted vegetables and top with *nökkelost* cheese for artistically prepared open-faced sandwiches.

Norwegian Crispbread Delight

4 pieces Kavli Norwegian crispbread
1 tablespoon mayonnaise
1/2 teaspoon spicy mustard
4 small leaves Bibb lettuce

4 thick slices *Jarlsberg* cheese
8 thin slices liverwurst
red onion rings

Spread crispbread with mayonnaise blended with mustard. Arrange the lettuce at one end, standing up slightly at end of bread. Place cheese on crispbread. Top with liverwurst and decorate with onion rings. Makes 4 sandwiches.

Salami and Fruit

rye bread or pumpernickel rye
butter
lettuce

salami
orange slices, with rind removed
strawberries, halved

Trim crusts and butter bread generously. Top with lettuce and 2 slices of salami, folded. Garnish with 2 or 3 slices of orange and strawberry halves.

Sliced Egg with Sardines

8 slices thin-style crispbreads
green leaf lettuce
2 7-ounce cans sardines, packed in
  oil, drained
2 small tomatoes, sliced

2 hard-cooked eggs, sliced
1 small onion, sliced and separated
  into rings
1/4 cup mayonnaise
1 tablespoon Dijon-style mustard

To make sandwiches: on each crispbread arrange a lettuce leaf; top with sardines, tomato slices, eggs, and onions. In a small bowl, blend mayonnaise and mustard; place a dollop of this mixture on top of each sandwich. Makes 8 open-faced sandwiches.

Salads — Vegetables

Beet and Onion Salad

Danish

2 20-ounce cans sliced beets,
    drained
1 medium-sized onion, sliced thinly
    into rings
Dressing:
1/4 cup salad oil
1/4 cup sugar
2 tablespoons vinegar

1 teaspoon lemon juice
1/4 teaspoon salt
1/8 teaspoon dry mustard
1/8 teaspoon paprika
1/8 teaspoon celery seed (optional)
pinch of garlic salt
dash of pepper

Mix together beets and onion rings in a shallow bowl. **Dressing:** Combine all dressing ingredients. Pour over beets and onion rings. Cover; refrigerate overnight.

—Olive Scotland Ferguson, Walnut, Iowa

From *Delectably Danish: Recipes and Traditions*

Cucumber Salad

Swedish

1 large cucumber
3 tablespoons water
4 tablespoons sugar
1/2 cup white vinegar

1/2 teaspoon salt
dash of pepper
few sprigs of fresh parsley

Wash cucumber and score lengthwise with a fork. Cut into thin slices and place in a shallow dish. Mix other ingredients together, except parsley, and pour over cucumbers. Chill 4 to 5 hours before serving. Garnish with parsley.

Cucumbers and Eggs

Swedish

4 hard-cooked eggs
1/3 cup finely chopped cucumber
2 tablespoons mayonnaise

salt
fresh parsley

Boil eggs and cut in half lengthwise. Remove yolks. In a bowl, mix together cucumber, mayonnaise, egg yolks, and salt. Fill halves of egg whites with yolk mixture. Garnish with a sprig of parsley.

Danish Beet Salad

1 16-ounce jar of pickled beets,
  sliced and drained

2 or 3 small apples, cut into thin slices
1/2 cup mayonnaise

In a large bowl, combine beets and apples. Stir in mayonnaise. Chill 4 to 5 hours before serving.

Finnish Potato Salad

3 pounds potatoes
2 cups mayonnaise
1/2 cup Dijon-style mustard
1/2 cup red wine vinegar
4 large scallions, sliced
1 large carrot, scraped, shredded

1 large rib of celery, finely diced
salt and ground black pepper to taste
8 small red cabbage leaves, rinsed
  and dried
1/4 cup chopped parsley

Scrub potatoes, cut in half, and cook in boiling water, about 20 minutes, until potatoes are tender. Drain and cool. In a large bowl, mix mayonnaise, mustard, and vinegar. Add scallions, carrot, celery, and salt and pepper. Dice potatoes, combine with mayonnaise mixture, and refrigerate. To serve *Voileipäpöytä* style, place the 8 red cabbage leaves, cup style, on a serving plate. Spoon salad onto red cabbage leaves and sprinkle with chopped parsley.　　—Finnish National Distillers (ALKO), Inc.

Herring Salad (*Sillsalad*)

Swedish

1 salt herring
5 to 6 potatoes, boiled, peeled, and diced
5 pickled beets, diced
2 small apples, peeled, cored, and diced
2 tablespoons chopped onion

5 tablespoons white vinegar
2 tablespoons sugar
1/4 teaspoon pepper
1/4 cup whipping cream, whipped
2 hard-cooked eggs, sliced
fresh parsley

Soak herring overnight; drain and slice into small cubes. Mix together potatoes, beets, peeled apples, and onions. Add vinegar, sugar, and pepper; mix thoroughly. Gradually fold in whipped cream. Place in a salad mold and refrigerate overnight. Unmold onto a platter and garnish with slices of hard-cooked egg and parsley.

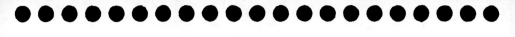

Mushroom Salad

Finnish

1 1/2 pounds frozen mushrooms,
  finely chopped
1 small leek, sliced

3/4 cup whipping cream, whipped
salt and pepper to taste

Combine chopped mushrooms, sliced leek, and whipped cream in a glass bowl. Mix ingredients together well and season to taste with salt and pepper.

Rosolli

Finnish

8 beets
8 carrots
6 potatoes
2 tart apples, peeled, cored, and
   finely chopped
2 onions, diced

2 dill pickles, diced
salt
Salad Cream:
1 3/4 cups whipping cream
2 teaspoons sugar
2 teaspoons white vinegar

Boil vegetables separately. Drain beef and reserve a little of the cooking liquid. Drain other vegetables and cool. Peel vegetables and onion and cut up fine. Combine cooked vegetables, apples, onions, and pickles. Season with salt. Toss and serve on large glass platter with salad cream in a separate dish.

Salad Cream: Whip cream until it is thick and stands in soft peaks. Add sugar and vinegar, and a little of the beet liquid to give cream a pink color. Mix well.

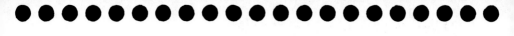

Salmon Salad Mold

Danish

2 packages lemon-flavored gelatin
2 cups boiling water
1/2 cup mayonnaise
1/2 cup half-and-half cream
1/2 cup pimiento cheese
1/2 teaspoon onion salt

1/2 cup cooked peas
1 1-pound can red salmon, flaked
3 hard-boiled eggs, sliced
1 cup diced celery
1/2 green pepper, chopped
1 stuffed olive

Dissolve gelatin in water. Add remaining ingredients, except eggs and olive; mix well. Use egg slices in bottom of fish-shaped mold for "backbone." Pour mixture into mold and chill. Unmold onto a bed of leaf lettuce. Slice stuffed olive and use for eyes.

—Esther Andersen, Dike, Iowa
From *Delectably Danish: Recipes and Traditions*

Smorgasalad

Norwegian

2 small tomatoes, thinly sliced
1 8 1/2-ounce can small whole
  potatoes, drained
1 8 1/2-ounce can sliced beets, drained
2 hard-cooked eggs, sliced
1/3 cup olive oil
3 tablespoons wine vinegar
3 tablespoons lime or lemon juice

1 clove garlic, crushed
1 teaspoon salt
1/2 teaspoon basil
pepper to taste
4 cups torn salad greens
1 3 3/4-ounce can of Spirit of Norway
  sardines in oil, drained

In a small bowl, combine first four ingredients. In another bowl, combine oil, vinegar, lime or lemon juice, garlic, salt, basil, and pepper. Mix thoroughly. Pour over vegetable and egg mixture. Chill and marinate at least 2 hours. Serve over salad greens. Garnish with sardines.

Broccoli Oscar

Norwegian

1/4 cup soy sauce
1 tablespoon vegetable oil
1 tablespoon sugar
1/4 teaspoon red pepper flakes
1 clove garlic, pressed
3 cups broccoli flowerettes, cooked
crisp and cooled

1 3 3/4-ounce can King Oscar
sardines in oil, drained
1 cup sliced carrots, cooked crisp (but
tender) and cooled
sesame seeds, for garnish

In a small bowl, combine soy sauce, oil, sugar, pepper flakes, and garlic. Arrange broccoli, sardines, and carrots in a shallow dish. Pour marinade over all. Chill and marinate for 30 minutes to 1 hour. Garnish with sesame seeds.

Creamed Cauliflower

Finnish

1 head cauliflower
water, salt
1 tablespoon butter
1 tablespoon white flour

milk
cooking liquid from cauliflower
1 teaspoon sugar
1 teaspoon salt

Cut cauliflower into small pieces; cook in salted water until tender. Drain and reserve liquid. Melt butter in a pan and add flour, stirring until smooth. Slowly add milk and cooking liquid; stir and cook for a few minutes until sauce begins to thicken. Place cooked cauliflower pieces in the sauce and simmer a few minutes longer. Add sugar and salt to taste.

—Ester Vuori Berg

Danish Braised Red Cabbage

1 medium-sized head red cabbage
4 tablespoons margarine
1 tablespoon sugar
1 teaspoon salt

1/3 cup water
1/3 cup white vinegar
1/4 cup currant jelly
2 tablespoons grated apple

Clean cabbage, removing the outer leaves, and cut cabbage in half. Shred each half with knife or in a food processor. Combine margarine, sugar, salt, water, and vinegar in large saucepan. When mixture comes to a boil, add shredded cabbage and toss thoroughly. Bring to a boil again; place in a casserole dish or roasting pan, cover tightly, and bake at 325° for 2 hours. Check liquid level periodically and add water if necessary. When cooked, stir in jelly and grated apple. Cover and continue baking for 10 minutes. Remove cover and let sit an additional 10 minutes before serving.

Danish Green Beans with Walnut Vinaigrette

1 clove garlic, minced
1/2 cup chicken broth, fresh or
canned
1 tablespoon olive oil
1 tablespoon balsamic or red wine
vinegar
1/3 cup walnuts, coarsely chopped

2 1/2 cups fresh green beans (ends
snipped), blanched and chilled
4 ounces Classic Saga blue cheese,
broken into chunks
ground black pepper
1 head Iceberg lettuce, leaves
separated

Combine first five ingredients to make vinaigrette. Pour over beans, add cheese, and toss lightly. Add pepper to taste. Cover and refrigerate for at least 1 hour. Remove from refrigerator about 1/2 hour before serving. Serve on the lettuce leaves. (Refrigerate any remaining lettuce for another use.)

Finnish Rutabaga Casserole

1 rutabaga
2 to 3 tablespoons butter

1/4 cup dry bread crumbs or 1/4 cup
  brown sugar

Pare and dice rutabaga and cook in water until soft. Drain, add butter, and mash well. Place mashed rutabaga in buttered casserole. Smooth top with spatula and then make indentations with bowl or spoon for design. Top with bread crumbs or brown sugar. Bake 35 to 40 minutes at 350° or until brown around edges.

—Ester Vuori Berg

Hasselback Potatoes

Swedish

8 medium-sized potatoes
5 tablespoons melted butter

salt (optional)
6 to 7 tablespoons bread crumbs
or Parmesan cheese

Preheat oven to 425°. Peel potatoes and slice down through each one at 1/8-inch intervals, being careful not to slice through the potato. Allow to dry on paper towel. Grease large baking dish and place potatoes in it, cut side up. Baste potatoes with the melted butter. Sprinkle with salt if desired. Bake for 25 minutes. Baste again, and sprinkle with bread crumbs or cheese. Bake for another 15 minutes, until slightly brown on top.

Hot Potato Salad

Danish

4 slices bacon
1 large onion, peeled and quartered
1/2 cup water
1 teaspoon sugar
1/2 teaspoon salt
2 tablespoons butter

3 tablespoons vinegar
6 to 8 cold, boiled, medium-sized
  potatoes
2 tablespoons cream
dash of pepper

Fry bacon, remove from fat, and drain on absorbent paper. In a large saucepan, boil onion in the 1/2 cup of water. Add sugar, salt, butter, and vinegar. Cook until onion is transparent. Slice potatoes and add slowly to the onion mixture, turning carefully to avoid breaking the potatoes. Add cream and pepper. Crumble bacon and mix lightly into the potato mixture. Serve hot.

—Julie Jensen McDonald

Jansson's Temptation

Swedish

2 tablespoons butter
5 medium potatoes, peeled and
    sliced
2 medium onions, sliced

1 3-ounce tin of anchovy fillets,
    drained, liquid reserved
liquid from anchovies and half-and-half
    to equal 3/4 cup

Grease a 2-quart casserole dish with the butter. Alternate layers of potatoes, onions, and anchovies, beginning and ending with potatoes. Pour half of the liquid over the layers and bake at 375° for about 30 minutes, or until the potatoes are lightly browned. Pour remaining liquid over all and continue baking for another 30 minutes, until potatoes are done.

Jarlsberg Pasta Primavera

Norwegian

2 tablespoons minced garlic
4 teaspoons sesame oil
4 tablespoons dried basil (or 1 cup fresh)
2 10-ounce packages frozen chopped spinach, thawed and squeezed dry
2 14 1/3-ounce cans of plum tomatoes with juice

2 cups chopped fresh plum tomatoes
1 pound *Jarlsberg* Lite cheese, shredded
1 pound short pasta, such as rotelli or spiralli, cooked *al dente* (slightly firm) and drained
1 cup pignoli nuts or chopped walnuts (optional)

Cook garlic in oil until golden. Add basil, spinach, and canned tomatoes. Simmer for 10 minutes. While cooking, chop tomatoes with a spoon. Add fresh tomatoes and cook 3 minutes longer. Add cheese. Toss with pasta. Garnish with nuts. Serve immediately.

95

Potatoes Browned in Sugar

Icelandic

2 pounds white potatoes
4 tablespoons butter

1/2 cup sugar

Select new potatoes, preferably small in size. If large, they should be cut in even pieces. Peel and boil. Brown the butter over low heat in a preheated saucepan. Add the sugar. When the mixture becomes frothy, add the potatoes. Turn, repeatedly, until the potatoes become well-coated and light brown.

—Embassy of Iceland, Washington, D.C.

Swedish Brown Beans

1 pound Swedish brown beans
3/4 cup brown sugar

1/2 cup red wine vinegar
2 teaspoons salt

Rinse beans in cold water. Place in pan, cover beans with cold water, and soak overnight. When ready to cook, add remaining ingredients and bring to a boil. Reduce heat; simmer several hours until beans are tender. Place in casserole dish and bake for about 30 minutes at 325°.

Note: Swedish brown beans can be found in gourmet food shops or the ethnic section of supermarkets. They can be grown in home gardens. Karen Berg Douglas says she has a friend whose garden provides a seasonal supply.

Turnip Casserole

Finnish

2 medium-sized turnips, peeled and
    sliced
boiling, lightly salted water
1 cup dry bread crumbs, divided
1 teaspoon salt

1 teaspoon nutmeg
3 tablespoons light corn syrup
1/2 cup cream, or half-and-half
2 large eggs, beaten
4 tablespoons butter, divided

Cook turnips for about 30 minutes in boiling, lightly salted water until tender. Drain well and mash until smooth. Preheat oven to 350°. Add 1/2 cup bread crumbs, salt, nutmeg, syrup, cream, eggs, and 3 tablespoons of the butter to the mashed turnips and mix well. Spoon into a lightly greased 2-quart casserole dish. Top with the remaining butter and bread crumbs. Bake for about 1 hour, until golden brown.

Warm Smoked Chicken Salad

8 cups shredded lettuce
1/4 cup parsley leaves
1 16-ounce can cling peaches in extra-light syrup
3 tablespoons each: vegetable oil and olive oil
1 shallot, minced
1 tablespoon Balsamic vinegar

1 teaspoon Dijon-style mustard
1/4 teaspoon thyme
1/2 pound small new potatoes, cooked until tender, sliced
6 ounces chicken or turkey, shredded
1 cup green beans, cooked
1/4 cup walnut pieces, toasted
4 to 6 ounces *Jarlsberg* Lite cheese, cut into thin strips

Arrange lettuce and parsley on plates. Set aside. Drain peaches. Heat 1 tablespoon vegetable oil in small frying pan. Stir in shallots. Cook until soft. Whisk in remaining vegetable oil, olive oil, vinegar, mustard, and thyme.

99

(continued)

Warm Smoked Chicken *(continued)*

Heat, whisking constantly, until dressing is hot. Stir in reserved peach slices, potatoes, shredded chicken, beans, and walnuts. Stir gently to coat well. Spoon mixture over lettuce on plate. Top with cheese strips to serve. Serves 6 to 8.

Meats — Fish

Swedish Lamb in Dill Sauce

2 pounds lamb, cubed
1 teaspoon salt
8 white peppercorns
1 onion, diced

1 leek, thinly sliced
2 carrots, diced
1/2 celery root, diced
1 bunch fresh dill

Sauce:

2 tablespoons butter
2 tablespoons flour
2 cups stock
1/2 teaspoon lemon juice
1 tablespoon white vinegar

2 teaspoons sugar
1/2 cup heavy cream
2 egg yolks
salt and pepper to taste
3 to 4 tablespoons finely chopped dill

Place meat, salt, and peppercorns into a casserole dish. Add enough water to cover

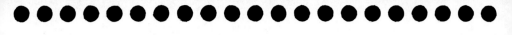

and bring to a boil. Skim excess fat. Add vegetables and dill. Simmer for 1 1/2 hours or until tender. Strain and boil stock down to 2 cups for sauce.

Sauce: In a saucepan, melt butter. Stir in flour until smooth. Gradually add stock and bring to a boil; boil 3 to 5 minutes. Add lemon juice, vinegar, and sugar. In a separate pan, cook cream and yolks over low heat until thickened (do not boil); remove from heat. Add salt, pepper, and dill. Stir mixture into the sauce. Serve the sauce with the lamb.

Traditional Icelandic Sunday Roast

1 leg of lamb
salt and pepper
4 tablespoons butter, softened

1 quart stock or hot water
flour

Wipe lamb with warm, damp cloth. Rub salt and pepper into the meat. Dot lamb with butter. Place into a greased roaster. Bake at 450° for 15 to 20 minutes. Reduce heat to 350°. Pour stock or water into the roaster, cover, and continue to roast for 15 minutes per pound, basting occasionally. When meat is done, skim excess fat from the drippings and add enough flour to make a smooth gravy.

—Embassy of Iceland, Washington, D.C.

104

Finnish Meatballs

3/4 cup soft bread crumbs
1 cup light cream or milk, divided
1 1/2 pounds lean ground beef, divided
1 onion, minced
1 egg, slightly beaten

1 1/2 teaspoons salt
1/2 teaspoon ground allspice
2 tablespoons butter
2 tablespoons flour
1 1/2 cups milk

Soak crumbs in 1/2 cup of the cream. Blend in beef, onion, egg, salt, and allspice. Shape into balls about 1 inch in diameter. Melt butter in skillet and brown the meatballs a few at a time. Shake pan to roll meatballs around so they brown evenly. After all meat is browned, remove from pan. Add flour to pan drippings. Stir and brown over medium heat. Slowly add the second 1/2 cup of cream and the milk, stirring to keep mixture smooth. Add water, if necessary, to thin out the gravy. Strain if desired. Return meatballs to pan. Cover and simmer 25 minutes.

—Finnish National Distillers (ALKO), Inc.

Icelandic *Rullupysla*

1 teaspoon ground cloves
2 tablespoons pepper
2 tablespoons onion powder

1 teaspoon ground allspice
3 pounds beef flank

Brine:

2 1/2 quarts boiling water
2 cups curing salt

1/2 teaspoon saltpeter

To prepare brine: stir salt and saltpeter into boiling water until dissolved.

To prepare meat: mix spices together. Trim fat and tough parts from meat. Cut flank into a large 1-inch-thick square. Sprinkle square with half the spice mix. Thinly slice remaining meat and place on square, sprinkling with remaining spice mix. Shape into a roll, sew ends, and seam. Place in brine 7 days. Remove from brine and boil 2 to 3 hours or until tender. Press between flat surfaces to cool. Slice and serve on bread.

Stuffed Cabbage

Swedish

1 medium-sized head green cabbage
Stuffing:
1 cup water
1/3 cup rice
1 pound ground chuck
1 teaspoon salt
1/2 cup milk

2 tablespoons butter
1/2 cup water or bouillon
salt and pepper to taste
Sauce:
2 tablespoons flour
1/2 cup cream or milk
salt and pepper to taste

Cook the cabbage in boiling salted water for 15 minutes. Carefully remove the leaves, one by one, and let dry. Bring 1 cup of water to a boil; stir in rice. Cover and cook on low heat for 18 minutes. Allow to cool. Combine the ground meat with the cooked rice; season with salt and pepper. Add the milk and mix well.

(continued)

Stuffed Cabbage *(continued)*

Remove coarse middle veins from each cabbage leaf; keep leaves intact. Spoon 2 tablespoons of meat mixture onto each flattened cabbage leaf, near the stem. Roll stem end over meat mixture once; fold in sides and roll to close. Rolls may be tied with string or fastened with toothpicks. Melt butter in a large frying pan or Dutch oven. Add the rolls with the opening side down; brown slowly on all sides. Do not crowd the pan; be careful when turning rolls so they keep their shape. When all rolls have been browned, add water or bouillon. Cover and cook over low heat for about 1 hour or until tender. Remove toothpicks or string. Place on serving dish.

Sauce: Thicken the pan juice with flour, if desired. Stir in 1/2 cup cream or milk. Heat, stirring until smooth. Season to taste and pour over the stuffed cabbage leaves.

—Gevalia Kaffe

Easy Swedish Sausage

Charlotte Jalkeus Anderson, an immigrant from Sweden, uses this recipe at Christmas, but recommends this special sausage as great for special occasions. She operates Anderson Butik and the Swedish Timber Cottage with her husband, Dean, in Lindsborg, Kansas.

1 pound ground beef
1 pound ground pork
3 or 4 boiled and mashed, cold potatoes
3 teaspoons salt
1/2 teaspoon ground white pepper

1/2 teaspoon ground cloves
1/2 teaspoon ground ginger
7 fluid ounces milk
1 tablespoon potato flour

Mix ground meat with mashed potatoes. Stir in remaining ingredients to make a nice dough. Let stand in the refrigerator 30 minutes. Make sausages 1 1/2 to 2 inches in diameter and not longer than the diameter of the pot to be used to boil the sausages.

(continued)

Easy Swedish Sausage *(continued)*

Wrap a piece of cling-wrap plastic two or three times around the meat. Make certain there is enough cling wrap at the ends. Tie a string around the ends and edges of the sausages. Put the sausages in boiling water and simmer 12 to 15 minutes. Don't boil. To serve warm, cut the cling wrappers on each end and press out the sausages. To serve cool, refrigerate in the plastic wrap. Remove wrap and cut into slices. Cooled sausages can be reheated, if desired.

Note: Uncooked sausage can be frozen, but not longer than 2 months. Cooked sausage or leftovers should not be frozen; keep in the refrigerator and reheat to serve.

Cabbage Rolls

Norwegian

1 15-ounce can sauerkraut
1 10 3/4-ounce can tomato soup, plus equal amount of water
8 ounces lightly seasoned pork sausage

rice, uncooked (equal to the volume of sausage)
1 medium-sized head cabbage, parboiled, leaves separated

Combine sauerkraut, tomato soup, and 1 can of water in a heavy saucepan. Bring to a boil and simmer gently. Mix equal volumes of rice and pork sausage. Put 1 tablespoon of mixture on cabbage leaf, roll up, and secure with string or toothpicks. Place cabbage balls in pot with sauerkraut and tomato soup mixture and simmer gently for about 4 hours. Check occasionally to see that there is enough liquid, so mixture will not burn.

—Betty Nelson Seegmiller, Decorah, Iowa
From *Notably Norwegian: Recipes and Traditions*

Danish Meatballs

1 pound ground pork
1 pound ground veal
1 teaspoon salt
1/2 teaspoon pepper

1 large onion, finely grated
1/2 cup flour
5 eggs
1 1/2 cups milk
2 to 3 tablespoons margarine

Mix meats with salt, pepper, and onion. Slowly add flour, eggs, and milk, mixing thoroughly. Form meat mixture into balls about 1 inch in diameter. Melt 2 to 3 tablespoons margarine in a skillet and add meatballs. Brown well, then turn down heat and fry slowly for about 5 minutes, or until done. Serves 8 to 10.

Danish Meat Patties

1/2 pound boneless veal
1/2 pound boneless pork
1/2 cup coarsely chopped onion
3 tablespoons flour
1 1/2 cups club soda

1 egg, well beaten
1 teaspoon salt
dash of pepper
6 tablespoons margarine

Grind veal, pork, and onion in a food processor. In a large mixing bowl, beat flour into ground meat mixture with a wooden spoon. Gradually add club soda, and continue to beat until mixture is light and fluffy. Add egg, salt, and pepper. Refrigerate for 1 hour. Shape mixture into oblong patties, about 1 inch thick. Melt margarine in a frying pan. When hot, add patties and fry for 10 to 12 minutes on each side, or until they are cooked through and no longer pink inside. Makes 8 to 10 patties.

Sautéed Veal Chops

Norwegian

3 tablespoons unsalted butter,
   divided
3 tablespoons vegetable oil, divided
1/4 cup finely chopped onion
4 large veal chops

Sauce:
1 cup sour cream
1/2 cup shredded *Gjetost* (Norwegian
   goat cheese)
salt and pepper to taste

Heat 1 tablespoon butter and 1 tablespoon oil in a heavy frying pan over medium heat. Add onions and cook for 3 to 5 minutes; remove from pan and set aside. Add remaining butter and oil to pan and heat. Pound veal chops to 1/4 inch thickness; fry over medium heat for 4 to 5 minutes on each side or until golden brown. Remove to platter and keep warm while you make the sauce.

Sauce: Remove excess fat from frying pan and add the cooked onions. Cook over high heat, stirring constantly, for 2 to 5 minutes. Lower heat and stir in sour cream and cheese, a little at a time. Add salt and pepper and stir until all the cheese has melted and the sauce is smooth. Return veal to frying pan and baste with the sauce, simmer uncovered for 1 to 2 minutes, and serve.

Danish Smoked Bacon with Apples and Onions

4 tablespoons butter, divided
1 pound Canadian bacon, sliced
2 large onions, sliced

3 medium-sized cooking apples:
   unpeeled, cored, and cut into
   1/2-inch wedges
black pepper

Melt half the butter in a skillet. Add bacon and fry until light brown. Remove to paper towel to drain. Add remaining butter to skillet and add onions. Fry until soft. Add apples; cover pan and simmer for 7 to 10 minutes or until apples are tender. Cut bacon into bite-sized pieces and return to pan. Simmer for 5 minutes. Season to taste. Place in casserole dish and serve.

Liver Loaf

Swedish

1 pound beef liver, sliced
2 large onions
1/2 pound salt pork
6 anchovy fillets
2 slices white bread

1/2 cup milk
1 egg
3 tablespoons white flour
1/2 teaspoon pepper
7 thin slices bacon

Place liver in pan, cover with boiling water, and simmer 5 minutes. Drain and cool. Remove skin and outer membrane. Put liver, onions, salt pork, anchovies, and bread through a food chopper twice. Add milk, egg, flour, and pepper. Mix thoroughly. Line loaf pan with slices of bacon. Add liver mixture and press firmly into pan. Bake at 375° for about 1 hour.

Icelandic Hot Dish

12 slices bread, diced, divided
1 to 2 tablespoons butter or
  margarine
1 cup diced ham
2 cups sliced mushrooms
1 cup mayonnaise
1/2 cup sour cream

1 tablespoon pickle relish
1 can tuna
3 hard-cooked eggs, diced
2 3-ounce cans small shrimp
salt and pepper to taste
4 egg whites
6 ounces cheese, shredded

Layer half the diced bread in a 9x13-inch baking dish. Melt butter in a skillet and fry ham and mushrooms together until mushrooms are soft. Pour contents of pan over bread crumb layer. Combine mayonnaise, sour cream, relish, tuna, hard-cooked eggs, shrimp, salt, and pepper. Spread half this mixture over the ham layer, then cover with other half of diced bread. Spread with remaining mayonnaise mixture. Beat egg whites until stiff and fold in cheese. Spread over the mayonnaise layer and bake at 350° for 45 minutes.

Danish Poached Fish

2 pounds whole, cleaned, cod
 or haddock
1 quart water
2 teaspoons salt

2 to 3 peppercorns
2 tablespoons white vinegar
4 whole allspice
1 bay leaf
thinly sliced cucumber, small tomato
 wedges, fresh parsley for garnish

In large saucepan, bring water, salt, peppercorns, vinegar, allspice, and bay leaf to a boil. Boil for 10 to 20 minutes. Add fish. Cover. Reduce heat and simmer slowly for 8 to 10 minutes. Remove from heat and allow fish to cool in water and spice mixture. Remove carefully to a serving platter and garnish with thinly sliced cucumbers, small tomato wedges, and parsley. Serves 4 to 6.

Lutefisk

Lutefisk *means "lye" fish. Prior to refrigeration, Norwegians preserved codfish using a lye process. A meat shop in Decorah, Iowa, sells over a ton of this holiday delicacy every year, imported from Norway. During the third weekend in October each year, the First Lutheran Church, Poulsbo, Washington, serves almost a ton of this specialty.* Lutefisk, *considered a rare delicacy in America, is hardly ever eaten in Norway today.*

2 pounds *lutefisk*   1/2 pound butter

Rinse fish in cold water. Cut into serving-sized pieces. Remove any scales. For cooking it is suggested that you tie fish in a piece of cheesecloth since it is tender and breaks apart easily. Place in a large saucepan with 4 or 5 quarts of cool salted water. Bring to a boil. Cook 10 minutes or until tender and translucent. Remove from water carefully. Serve with melted butter. Makes 4 servings.

Poached Fish

Norwegian

3 pounds frozen fillets of cod or haddock (defrosted)
boiling salted water

melted butter with chopped parsley, or Hollandaise sauce
tomato wedges for garnish

Cut each fillet into individual servings. Drop fillets into a kettle of boiling salted water. Bring to a boil again, reduce heat, and simmer for 10 to 12 minutes. When done, lift fillets out with a slotted spoon. Save the stock to make a Hollandaise sauce, if desired. Serve with fish on a warm platter. Decorate with tomato wedges.

—Sigrid Marstrander
From *Time-Honored Norwegian Recipes*

Salmon with Finlandia Beurre Blanc

2 cups Finlandia vodka
1 cup fresh-squeezed lime juice,
   plus a wedge of lime
1/4 cup shallots, minced
1/4 cup heavy cream
1 pound butter, chilled, cut into cubes

salt
white pepper
6 5-ounce pieces of Norwegian salmon
1/2 jalapeño: charred, peeled, and minced
2 tablespoons cilantro, minced
salt and pepper to taste

In a saucepan over high heat, cook Finlandia vodka, lime juice, and shallots until syrupy and reduced to about 1 tablespoon (about 15 minutes). Add cream; stir and cook until thickened. Reduce heat and whip in butter, a few cubes at a time. Season with salt, white pepper, and a squeeze of lime. Place jalapeño on a long fork and hold directly over heat until skin is charred and easily removed. Grill salmon about 3 minutes on each side or until done. Whip minced jalapeño and cilantro into sauce and ladle sauce over the salmon.

—Created by Chef Martin Garcia

Michael's Restaurant, Santa Monica, California

Desserts

Cakes:

Cookies:

Pastries, Puddings, and More:

Apple Cake

Danish

2 cups bread, cake, or a combination
  of crumbs
3 tablespoons sugar, divided
1/2 cup butter

2 1/2 cups tart applesauce
1 cup whipping cream
red jelly or jam (for decoration)

Brown crumbs in skillet with 1 tablespoon sugar and the butter. Arrange crumb mixture and applesauce in alternate layers in a glass serving dish. Chill in refrigerator. Whip the cream and 2 tablespoons of sugar for topping. Decorate with dabs of the jelly or jam. For a crunchy texture, serve immediately. Advance preparation will create a moist blend of layers.

—Elisabeth Wood, Rock Island, Illinois

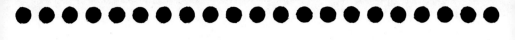

Icelandic Cake

1/2 cup butter, softened
1 cup plus 1 tablespoon sugar
1 cup milk
2 1/2 cups flour

2 1/2 teaspoons baking powder
2 cups raisins
dash of ground cardamon
3 egg whites, well-beaten

Cream butter and sugar together. Slowly add milk, flour, and baking powder. Add raisins and cardamon and beat well. Fold in well-beaten egg whites. Pour batter into a 9x13-inch pan and bake at 350° for about 45 minutes, or until cake tests done.

Icelandic Prune Cake

1 cup butter
2 cups sugar
4 eggs
1/2 cup sour cream

1 teaspoon baking soda
1 teaspoon baking powder
5 to 6 cups plus 1 teaspoon flour

Filling:
water for cooking
3 pounds prunes

1 cup sugar
1 teaspoon ground cardamon
vanilla

Cream butter and sugar; blend in eggs and sour cream. Sift together dry ingredients and blend into butter mixture. Knead slightly. Chill for at least 1 hour. Divide dough into 10 parts. On a floured surface, roll out each part of dough to fit the bottom of a 9-inch round cake pan. Place dough in greased pans and bake at 350° for 10 minutes. Cool and stack like cookies.

126

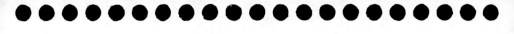

Filling: Cover prunes with water and cook until tender. Reserve 1/2 cup of the cooking liquid. Pit and mash prunes. Add the 1/2 cup of cooking liquid and the sugar. Cook until mixture thickens. Add 1 teaspoon cardamon and vanilla to taste.

Assembly: Use 5 of the baked layers for each cake. Spread 2/3 cup of filling between each layer. Let stand for 24 hours before serving.

—Fred Bjornson, Cedar Rapids, Iowa

Lingonberry Cake

Finnish

1/4 cup butter or margarine
3/4 cup granulated sugar
1 large egg
1 cup white flour

1 teaspoon baking powder
1/8 teaspoon salt
1 1/2 cups preserved lingonberries
1/4 cup granulated sugar

Preheat oven to 350°. In a large bowl, cream together butter and sugar until smooth. Add egg and continue beating until mixture is smooth and thick. In a separate bowl, sift together flour, baking powder, and salt. Gradually add flour mixture to first mixture, and stir until smooth. Pour batter into a buttered 13x9x2-inch baking pan and spread evenly. Top batter with lingonberries and sprinkle with sugar. Bake for about 30 minutes, until brown at edges. Serve warm, topped with a dab of whipped cream.

Skanor's Almond Cake

Swedish

Batter:
5 egg whites
1 cup powdered sugar
2/3 cup ground almonds

Topping:
3 egg yolks
1 cup light cream (half-and-half)
3/4 cup granulated sugar
1 1/2 tablespoons butter or margarine
1/2 cup toasted sliced almonds

Batter: Preheat oven to 400°. Beat egg whites until stiff. Slowly add powdered sugar and ground almonds. Butter an 8-inch cake pan and dust with flour. Pour in batter and bake for about 15 minutes. Cool and remove to serving plate.

Topping: Mix together egg yolks, cream, sugar, and butter in a 2-quart pan. Heat mixture to boiling, stirring continuously. Reduce heat and simmer until it begins to thicken. Pour into bowl and cool. Spread topping over almond cake just before serving. Garnish with toasted sliced almonds.

Swedish Nutcake

Cake:
3/4 cup sugar
2 eggs
2 cups flour
2 teaspoons baking soda
1 20-ounce can crushed pineapple,
　with juice
1/2 cup chopped nuts

Frosting:
7 tablespoons margarine, softened
8 ounces cream cheese, softened
1 teaspoon vanilla
1 3/4 cups powdered sugar
1/2 cup chopped nuts

Cake: In a large bowl, mix sugar and eggs together; mix in flour, baking soda, and pineapple; mix well. Stir in nuts. Pour batter into a 9x13-inch greased and floured baking pan. Bake at 350° for about 35 minutes, or until brown. Allow to cool.

Frosting: Mix margarine and cream cheese together; add vanilla, powdered sugar, and chopped nuts. Mix well. Spread over cooled cake.

Tosca Cake

Swedish

Cake:
2 eggs
2/3 cup sugar
3/4 cup flour
1 teaspoon baking powder
2 tablespoons cream
1/2 cup melted and cooled butter

Topping:
4 tablespoons butter
1/2 cup blanched and slivered
  almonds
3 tablespoons sugar
1 tablespoon flour
1/2 tablespoon cream

Cake: Beat the eggs. Add the sugar and beat for a few minutes. Mix in the flour, baking powder, cream, and melted butter. Pour the batter into a greased, floured 9-inch round cake pan. Bake at 350° for about 20 to 25 minutes, or until half-done.

Topping: Melt the butter for the topping. Mix in almonds, sugar, flour, and cream. Let come to a boil. Spread over cake and bake another 10 to 15 minutes.

—Embassy of Sweden, Washington, D.C.

Finnish Star Cookies

1 1/2 cups flour
1 cup butter, softened and divided
1/2 cup water
cream and sugar for top

Date Filling:
1 cup sugar
1/2 pound dates, finely cut
1 cup water

Filling: Mix ingredients together and cook slowly until thickened. Cool.

Dough: Mix 1/2 cup of the butter with the flour. Add water slowly while stirring to make a smooth dough. When well-mixed, chill dough thoroughly. On a floured surface, roll out to 1/8-inch thickness. Spread half the rolled-out dough with some of the remaining butter; fold over buttered half and roll again to 1/8-inch thickness. Repeat until all butter is used. Then roll dough out until thin. Cut into 2 1/2-inch squares. Cut a 1-inch slash in each corner. Place a spoonful of date mixture in the center of each square. Fold opposite corners to center of filling. Brush with cream and sprinkle with sugar. Bake at 375° for 5 to 7 minutes.

Grandma's Best Ginger Cookies

Finnish

1 cup dark corn syrup
2 teaspoons ground cinnamon
2 teaspoons ground ginger
2 teaspoons ground cloves
1 tablespoon grated orange rind

1 1/4 cups margarine
1 1/4 cups sugar
3 eggs
7 cups flour (approximately)
3 teaspoons baking soda

Boil the syrup, spices, and grated orange rind; add the margarine and beat until the mixture is cool. Beat sugar and eggs together. Mix soda with 3 cups of the flour, then combine with the syrup-margarine mixture. Add whipped egg mixture and rest of the flour (enough to make a stiff dough). Do not knead the final mixture. Cover with plastic wrap and cool overnight. On a floured surface, roll out the dough, cut into shapes, and bake at 400° for about 10 minutes. Makes 200.

—From *Entertaining the Finnish Way*

Icelandic Rolled Cookies

2/3 cup sugar
1 cup butter, softened
1 1/4 to 2 cups flour

1/2 teaspoon baking powder
1 egg yolk, beaten
sugar for sprinkling

Cream sugar and butter together. Combine the 1 1/4 cups flour and the baking powder. Add to the butter mixture. Mix well. Roll out on a floured surface and cut into desired shapes. Place on a greased baking sheet, brush with the beaten egg yolk, and sprinkle with the sugar. Bake at 350° for 10 to 12 minutes, or until lightly browned.

—Fred Bjornson

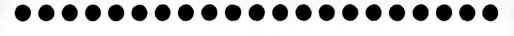

Krumbles

Finnish

Batter:
1 cup brown sugar
1 cup margarine, softened
1 egg
1 teaspoon vanilla
2 cups flour
2 cups oatmeal

Topping:
8 ounces dates, chopped
3/4 cup sugar
1/8 cup water (approximately)

Batter: Mix all batter ingredients together well. Put 3/4 of the batter on a small cookie sheet with edges; pat into place.

Prepare topping: Mix together all topping ingredients. Bring to a boil and cook about 2 to 3 minutes. Cool slightly.

Assembly: Cover oatmeal batter with date mixture. Crumble remaining oatmeal batter on top of date topping. Bake about 15 to 20 minutes at 350°. Cut into bars.

Pepparkakor
Swedish

1 cup butter
1 1/2 cups sugar
1 tablespoon dark corn syrup
2 teaspoons cinnamon

2 teaspoons ginger
1 teaspoon cloves
1 large egg
1 teaspoon baking soda
2 1/2 cups sifted flour

Mix butter, sugar, syrup, and spices together. Add egg and beat well. Fold in baking soda and flour slowly, until dough is easy to handle. On a lightly floured surface, roll dough out into a thin sheet and cut with a heart-shaped cookie cutter. Preheat oven to 350°. Place cookies on cookie sheet and bake for 5 to 7 minutes or until golden brown. Remove from cookie sheet and cool.

Pebernødder

Danish

2 1/2 cups flour
1 teaspoon ground cardamon
1 teaspoon cinnamon
1/4 teaspoon white pepper

1 cup butter, softened
1/2 cup sugar
2 eggs
rind of 1 lemon, grated

Sift together flour, cardamon, cinnamon, and pepper. Cream butter and sugar; add eggs and grated lemon rind. Add dry mixture to butter mixture. Knead until smooth dough is formed. Refrigerate for 1 hour. Shape dough into small balls and place on a greased baking sheet. Bake at 325° for about 10 to 12 minutes, or until golden brown.

Sarah Bernhardt

Danish

This dessert, a chocolate-topped macaroon base with chocolate truffle filling, was named for the French actress upon her visit to Copenhagen in 1880.

Macaroon base:
1 cup sugar
3 1/2 ounces almond paste
2 or 3 egg whites

Chocolate truffle filling:
4 ounces unsweetened chocolate
2 cups whipped cream

Macaroon base: Mix almond paste and sugar together. Add egg whites and blend to a porridge-like consistency. Divide mixture into approximately 10 parts and place on baking sheet. Bake 20 minutes at 350°.

Chocolate truffle filling: Melt chocolate. Blend half of the melted chocolate into the whipped cream; chill, then spread chilled chocolate mixture on macaroon base. Dip the top of the confection into the remaining chocolate. Refrigerate for 2 or 3 hours.

—Conditoriet La Glace, Copenhagen, Denmark

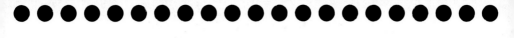

Swedish Cream Wafers

Wafers:
1/3 cup soft butter
1/3 cup thick cream
2 cups sifted all-purpose flour

Filling:
1/4 cup soft butter
3/4 cup powdered sugar
1 egg yolk
1 teaspoon vanilla

Wafers: Combine all ingredients together in a large bowl. Mix well and chill. Roll out half the dough to 1/8-inch thickness. Using a fluted cutter, cut into rounds. Keep remaining dough cool. Place the rounds on sugar-covered waxed paper. Turn to coat both sides. Prick each round four times with the tines of a fork. Place on ungreased cookie sheet and bake at 375° for 7 to 9 minutes. Cool and put 2 rounds together with the filling.

Filling: Combine all ingredients. Spread over cooled wafer and top with another.

—Luela Maki, Ely, Minnesota

Vanilla Wreaths (Spritz)

Danish

1 1/2 cups butter
2 1/4 cups sugar
2 eggs, beaten

1 1/2 teaspoons vanilla
3 1/2 cups flour
1/2 cup finely chopped almonds

Cream butter and sugar together in a mixing bowl. Add the rest of the ingredients and mix until dough is smooth. Chill dough slightly, then put dough into a cookie press. On a greased cookie sheet, press lengths of dough into small wreath shapes (about 1 inch in diameter). Bake at 325° until slightly brown, about 10 to 12 minutes. Makes about 150 cookies.

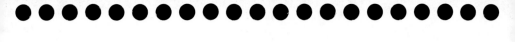

Asa's Kleinur

Icelandic

1 cup brown sugar
1 cup sugar
2 eggs, beaten
1 cup buttermilk
1/2 cup cream
2 teaspoons ground cardamon

1 teaspoon baking soda
2 teaspoons baking powder
1 teaspoon salt
5 to 6 cups flour, divided
oil for frying

Combine first 5 ingredients. Sift together cardamon, baking soda, baking powder, salt, and 5 cups flour. Add to the buttermilk mixture with enough flour to make a soft dough. Turn onto a floured surface and roll out to 1/4-inch thickness. Cut into 1x3-inch strips. Cut a slit in the center of each strip. Twist one end of the strip through the hole. Heat oil for deep-frying, as if for doughnuts, and fry *kleinur* until golden brown.

—Fred Bjornson

Fattigmand

Norwegian

4 egg yolks
4 tablespoons sugar
4 tablespoons cream
4 tablespoons butter, melted
1 tablespoon lemon juice

2 cups flour
1/2 teaspoon ground cardamon
oil for deep-frying
powdered sugar for sprinkling

Beat egg yolks until light and fluffy. Add sugar, cream, melted butter, and lemon juice and beat well. Stir in flour and add cardamon; mix well to form a smooth dough. Roll dough out into thin sheets on lightly floured pastry cloth. Cut into diamond shapes, then cut a slit in the center of each diamond and pull one corner through. Deep-fry in hot oil (about 350°) until brown. Drain on absorbent paper. When cool, sprinkle with powdered sugar.

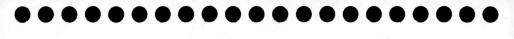

Icelandic Pancakes

3 cups flour
3 tablespoons butter, melted
1/2 teaspoon baking soda

1/2 teaspoon baking powder
1 teaspoon vanilla flavoring
2 1/2 cups milk
4 egg whites, stiffly beaten

In a large mixing bowl, mix all ingredients together. Add stiffly beaten egg whites last. If mixture is too thick, add a little more milk, about 1/4 cup. Bake on a hot griddle, about 2 to 3 minutes on each side. Remove from griddle; spread with jam, jelly, or whipped cream. Fold into triangles. Serve warm.

Norwegian Cones

1 cup melted butter
1 cup sugar
3 eggs
1 cup cream

1/2 teaspoon salt
2 cups flour
1/2 teaspoon grated lemon rind
1/2 teaspoon lemon juice

Mix ingredients in a large bowl. If dough will not hold together, add a little milk to the mixture. Place about 1 to 2 tablespoons of the batter in a hot *krumkake* iron and bake until each side is a light golden brown. Remove from iron and quickly roll the *kake* around a wooden cone-shaped baking stick to form the cone shape.

Rosettes

Swedish

2 eggs, slightly beaten
2 tablespoons sugar
1/4 teaspoon salt
1 cup milk

1 cup flour
1 teaspoon melted butter
oil for frying
powdered sugar for dusting

Add sugar and salt to beaten eggs. Alternately add flour and milk. Then add melted butter, beating only until dough is smooth. Heat oil in a frying pan. Dip rosette iron in hot oil, drain slightly, and dip into batter. Fry rosette for about 1 to 2 minutes, or until golden brown. Loose and remove rosette with fork and place on absorbent paper to drain. When cool dust rosettes with powdered sugar.

Sand Tarts

Norwegian

1 pound butter
1/4 pound margarine
1 1/2 cups sugar
1 egg

2 teaspoons almond extract
2 cups shredded coconut
2 tablespoons cream, or half-and-half
5 cups flour
filling if desired

Apricot Cream:
6 ounces dried apricots
1 cup sugar
1 pint whipping cream
1/2 teaspoon almond flavoring

Fillings

Almond Paste:
4 egg whites
1 cup ground almonds or walnuts
1 cup powdered sugar
1/2 teaspoon almond flavoring

Tarts: Cream together butter, margarine, and sugar. Add eggs, almond extract, coconut, and cream. Slowly add flour and mix thoroughly. Refrigerate dough until cool. With thumbs, press dough into small fluted tins. Bake at 350° until light brown, about 10 to 12 minutes. Allow cookies to cool in tins. To unmold, tap bottom of tin gently with a knife handle. Serve plain or fill with Apricot Cream or Almond Paste. (If using **Almond Paste,** do not bake tarts before filling.)

Apricot Cream: Cover apricots with water. Boil gently in uncovered saucepan for about 30 minutes. Add sugar during the last 5 minutes. Mash and chill. Whip cream into stiff peaks. Add mashed apricots and almond flavoring. Fill baked tart shells just before serving.

Almond Paste: Beat egg whites until stiff. Add powdered sugar, ground nuts, and flavoring. Fill unbaked tarts. Bake at 325° for about 20 minutes. Allow to cool in tins before unmolding.

Apple Cobbler Kavli

6 cups sliced tart baking apples
1/2 cup coarsely chopped pecans
1/2 cup raisins
3/4 cup sugar
2 tablespoons flour
3/4 teaspoon ground cinnamon, divided
1/8 teaspoon salt

5 tablespoons melted butter, divided
2 tablespoons lemon juice
1 teaspoon vanilla extract
1 1/2 cups coarsely crumbled thick Norwegian *Kavli* crispbread
1/8 teaspoon ground nutmeg
sweetened whipped cream or ice cream

In a large bowl, combine apples, pecans, raisins, sugar, flour, 1/2 teaspoon cinnamon, salt, 2 tablespoons of the butter, lemon juice, and vanilla extract. Toss to blend. Spoon into a buttered 8-inch square baking dish. Bake at 375° for 30 minutes.

Meanwhile, combine *Kavli* crumbs, remaining 3 tablespoons butter, 1/4 teaspoon cinnamon, and the nutmeg. Spoon over apple mixture; bake 5 minutes longer or until top is golden and apples are tender. Serve warm or cold, topped with sweetened whipped cream or ice cream. Makes 6 to 8 servings.

Baked Apples with Warm *Gjetost* Rum Sauce

6 baking apples, cored
3/4 cup dried fruit, diced (about the
    size of raisins)
1/4 teaspoon ground ginger
1/4 teaspoon cinnamon

Sauce:
1/2 cup evaporated skim milk
2 teaspoons flour
1/2 cup shredded *Gjetost* cheese
1 tablespoon brown sugar
1/2 teaspoon vanilla
2 teaspoons rum

Combine dried fruit, ginger, and cinnamon; stuff into center of each apple. Arrange apples in a baking pan with a small amount of water (about 1/4 inch) in the bottom of the pan. Cover with aluminum foil and bake at 350° for 30 to 45 minutes, until soft.

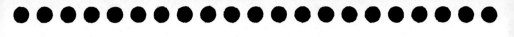

While apples are baking, prepare sauce: In the top of a double boiler, heat milk and flour, stirring constantly until slightly thickened. Stir in cheese, sugar, and vanilla until smooth. Stir in rum. Makes about 1/2 cup of sauce. Serve apples with sauce poured over the top and sides.

Fruit Sago Soup

Danish

8 cups water	1 cup pitted prunes
1/2 cup sago or 1/2 cup instant tapioca	1/2 cup raisins
	1/2 cup fruit juice (peach or pear)
1 stick cinnamon	1/4 cup sugar

Bring water to a boil; add sago, cinnamon stick, prunes, and raisins. Simmer until sago is clear. Add juice and sugar. More juice or sugar may be added to taste. Makes 8 servings.

Note: Sago is a thickening agent used widely in Scandinavian countries. It must be soaked an hour, then drained before using. It is not readily available in most U.S. supermarkets, but tapioca may be used as a substitute.

—Myrtle Petersen, Harlan, Iowa

Gjetost Dessert Salad

2 cups melon balls
2 cups halved strawberries
1 banana, sliced
1 grapefruit, sectioned
1 cup *Gjetost* cheese, cut into small
  cubes

1/3 cup mayonnaise
1 tablespoon honey
1 tablespoon olive oil
1 tablespoon orange juice
grated orange rind
1/3 cup heavy cream, whipped
1/4 cup toasted coconut

In a bowl, combine fruits and *Gjetost* cheese; toss to blend. In a small bowl, blend mayonnaise, honey, olive oil, orange juice, and grated orange rind. Fold in whipped cream and coconut. Spoon over fruit combination. Toss to blend. Makes 6 servings.

Norwegian Prune Pudding

1 pound prunes
2 cups cold water
1 cup sugar

1 1/2 cups boiling water
1/3 cup cornstarch
1 teaspoon lemon juice
2 egg whites, beaten

In a saucepan, soak prunes in cold water for several hours; then cook prunes in the same water until soft. Cool and cut prunes into small pieces. Return prunes to heat; add cinnamon, sugar, and boiling water. Simmer 10 minutes. Mix cornstarch with a little water and add to prune mixture; continue to cook until mixture is thickened. Add lemon juice and beaten egg whites. Mix well and serve.

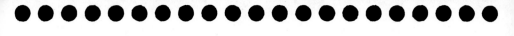

Rice Pudding

Danish

1 cup rice, uncooked	8 tablespoons sugar
4 cups milk	1/2 teaspoon salt
1 1/2 to 2 envelopes unflavored gelatin	2 cups whipped cream
1/2 cup water	2 teaspoons vanilla
	1/2 cup chopped almonds (optional)

Cook rice in milk; bring to a boil and simmer for about 18 minutes. Soften gelatin in 1/2 cup of water. Add softened gelatin, sugar, and salt to the cooked rice. Cool. Add whipped cream and vanilla. Put into a bowl and chill until fairly firm. Serve with a cold fruit sauce, or use a Danish dessert pudding mix for an excellent sauce. Sprinkle with nuts if desired.

—Thora Mae Andersen, Solvang, California

Snow Pudding

Finnish

To make an authentic snow pudding, a deep snow bank is desired, but any other method of keeping the bowl chilled while whipping will suffice to make this light and fluffy pudding.

water for cooking
1 cup cranberries
1 cup sugar

1/2 cup uncooked farina or
   Cream of Wheat
1 1/2 tablespoons cornstarch

In enough water to cover, boil cranberries until soft. Drain; reserve a little of the cooking liquid. Press cooked cranberries through a sieve until most of the pulp is mashed through the sieve. Return the purée to the pan; add sugar and slowly

sprinkle in farina or Cream of Wheat. Cook 20 minutes over low heat, stirring occasionally with a wooden spoon. Make a paste of cornstarch and a little of the cooking liquid; add to the puréed mixture. Cook to a sauce-like consistency. Place mixture in a large bowl. Pudding will increase greatly in volume while mixing, so use a bowl about double the volume of ingredients before whipping. Take outside and place in a snowbank, so snow surrounds the bowl. Whip with a wire whisk, serrated spoon, or hand beater for about 20 minutes or until mixture becomes light pink in color. Return to the refrigerator and chill thoroughly before serving. Serve with milk or cream, if desired.

—Ester Vuori Berg

Swedish Nuts

2 egg whites
1 cup sugar
4 cups pecans, walnuts, or almonds

1/2 cup butter or margarine
pinch of salt

Beat egg whites until frothy. Add sugar a little at a time and continue to beat until stiff. Fold in nuts. Melt butter or margarine in a 13x9x2-inch cake pan; add a pinch of salt. Spread meringue mixture over the butter and bake at 350° for 30 minutes. Stir mixture about every 10 minutes, spooning butter over the nuts. When done, the nuts should be coated with a caramel-like coating. Spread on waxed paper to cool.

BOOKS BY MAIL Stocking Stuffers POSTPAID You may mix titles. One book for $9.95; two for $16; three for $23; four for $28; twelve for $75 *(Prices subject to change.)* Please call 1-800-728-9998

æbleskiver and More
   A Sampling of Danish Recipes
American Gothic Recipes
Cherished Czech Recipes
Czech & Kolache Recipes
   & Sweet Treats
Dandy Dutch Recipes
Dear Danish Recipes
Fine Finnish Foods
Great German Recipes
License to Cook Italian Style
Norwegian Recipes
Pleasing Polish Recipes
Quality Czech Mushroom Recipes
Quality Dumpling Recipes
Recipes from Ireland

Savory Scottish Recipes
Scandinavian Holiday Recipes
Scandinavian Smorgasbord Recipes
Scandinavian Style Fish and Seafood Recipes
Scandinavian Sweet Treats
Slavic Specialties
Splendid Swedish Recipes
Ukrainian Recipes
License to Cook Arizona Style
License to Cook Iowa Style
License to Cook Minnesota Style
License to Cook New Mexico Style
License to Cook Texas Style
License to Cook Wisconsin Style
Waffles, Flapjacks, Pancakes....
      from Scandinavia and around the World

PENFIELD BOOKS • 215 BROWN STREET • IOWA CITY, IA 52245-5842